About the Author

MICHAEL MCTAGUE has been studying poetry for many years before he started creating poetry. He completed his doctoral dissertation at the University of Iowa by comparing translations of *Beowulf*. His studies span medieval and modern literature as well as Old Norse, Dante and Latin works. Over the years, he has taught many courses in literature, writing and business. He is the author of *The Businessman in Literature: Dante to Melville*, published by The Philosophical Library.

A New York native, his poems draw from a variety of experiences in and out of the largest city in the US. Dr. McTague has taught many college-level courses. He also studied Poetics with the Pulitzer Prize-winning American poet James Wright.

He spends a good deal of his time working at a private equity firm in New York. In this role, he has worked with companies in energy, pharmaceuticals, medical equipment, travel services, mining, higher education and other industries to secure financing. He has written numerous articles on business and contributes to Equities.com. You can find him on an Amazon author's page. In 2020, he published *Secrets of Effective Business Plans.* In 2021, his first book of poems, *Poems from the Top of the World* was published by Vanguard Press

Most photos were taken by the author, others are Royalty free photos taken from the internet.

This is a work of fiction. Names, characters, businesses, places, events and incidents are either the products of the author's imagination or used in a fictitious manner. Any resemblance to actual persons, living or dead, or actual events is purely coincidental.

FROM THE EDGE OF EUROPE TO
YANKEE STADIUM

Michael McTague

FROM THE EDGE OF EUROPE TO YANKEE STADIUM

Vanguard Press

VANGUARD PAPERBACK
© Copyright 2022
Michael McTague
The right of Michael McTague to be identified as author of this work has been asserted by him in accordance with the Copyright, Designs and Patents Act 1988.
All Rights Reserved

No reproduction, copy or transmission of this publication may be made without written permission.
No paragraph of this publication may be reproduced, copied or transmitted save with the written permission of the publisher, or in accordance with the provisions of the Copyright Act 1956 (as amended).
Any person who commits any unauthorised act in relation to this publication may be liable to criminal prosecution and civil claims for damages.

A CIP catalogue record for this title is available from the British Library.
ISBN 978-1-80016-529-8
Vanguard Press is an imprint of
Pegasus Elliot Mackenzie Publishers Ltd.
www.pegasuspublishers.com
First Published in 2022
Vanguard Press
Sheraton House Castle Park
Cambridge England
Printed & Bound in Great Britain

Contents

The Edge of Europe 11

The Pastry Job 14

Yankee Stadium Then and Now 17

The Science Fair 21

Kind Hearts are More than Coronets 22

Penicillin Losing its Strength 25

More Horseradish 28

The Great Toshi 33

A Viking Journey 35

Old Toys 39

From the Wasteland 43

Benignity 45

The Deadline 48

Bad Times for Theologians and Investors 51

E Pluribus Unum 57

Times Past 59

The Edge of Europe

The Birds of Northern Iceland perch on the extreme western
Tip of Europe in the crevices of a carved mountain.
Rivaled by the Cliffs of Moher, Latrabjarg features
A short transit to America, few visitors.

Not very far north of Thingvellir,
Where modern democracy came into being
In a land ruled by the Viking
Man splitters. Nifty with axe and spear.
Little art. Old technology. Relying on raw power.
And yet, they learned to speak with reason and wisdom.
As sheep grazed safely next to Lake Thingvallavatn.

The pain of Europe oozes north and west
Coming to a head at Iceland's western point.
Pushed away from their home by a range of fears.
Symbolic of Europe's millions, hoping for new land
These winged inhabitants lean toward the new world.
Venturing no more than half a mile westward
Over the ocean and its cold, stormy blasts.

A strange alliance links these residents
Puffins protect their windswept perches.
Terns possess enormous strength for flight
These species reveal the inbred instincts
Of all who depart the land of their birth
Holding on, never abandoning the old country.

Look closely at the colourful puffin
Head tilted, prominent eye, large beak,
Fixed intently on any nearby human.
Investigate their rocky domicile

At the far end, it comes to a point
Showing the way to a new land.

The birds yearn for departure
Remaining far above the strife
Swooping briefly to the ocean roar.
Moving slightly westward but no farther.
Staying with the old, the unforgiving.
And for all who seek a full release, gently beckoning
Glancing toward the terrifying rambunctious
Melting pot and a new beginning.

The Pastry Job

Wiping the ashes from our foreheads,
We feast on cannoli and raspberry tarts
The Ferrara's box top bent open makes it all just so
Fingerprints from powder and icing cover the label.
Gobs of whipped cream for the cappuccino
Served in Capo di Monte cups and saucers
Adorned with a sketch of Romulus and Remus
All arranged neatly on the old oak table.

Cousin Tony's job is the antipasto
For the piccolini, soda and gelato.
Rosa will bring the Fra Angelico
Perfect with the green glasses from Murano
A pot of Darjeeling for our Irish neighbour, Mrs O'Shea.
Ash Wednesday is such a special day.

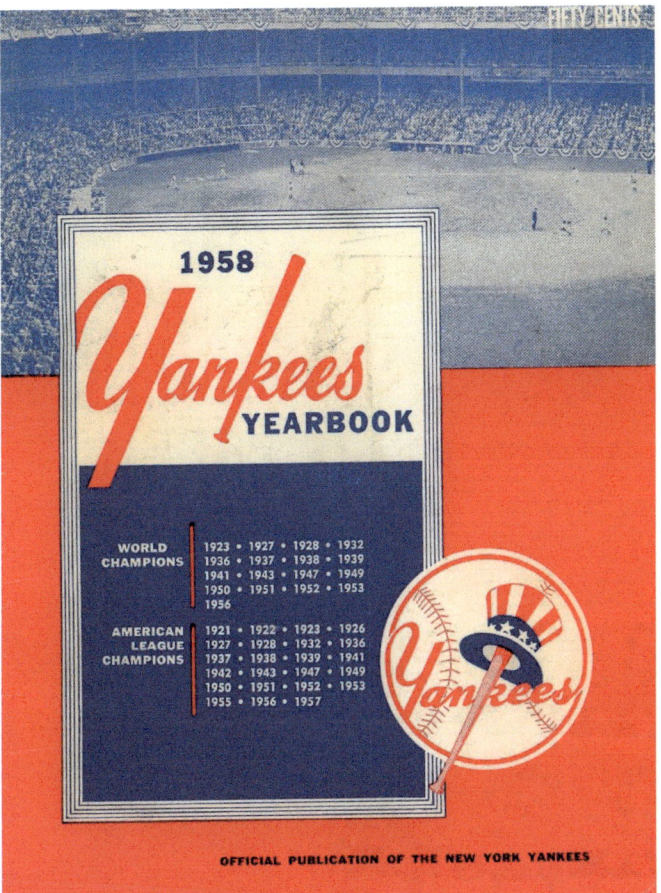

YOGI BERRA

CATCHER 8

Born, May 12, 1925 at St. Louis, Mo. Resides at Tenafly, N. J. Height—5'8". Weight—192. Bats left. Throws right. Married and father of three boys, Lawrence, Jr. (8), Timmy (6) and Dale (1). Color of hair, brown. Color of eyes, brown.

If the Yanks' veteran catcher can hit 20 or more home runs this year, it will mark the 10th straight season he has accomplished this feat. In fact, every time Yogi hits one out of the park, he sets a new mark for receivers. Going into the 1958 season, Berra had rapped 262 round-trippers. Despite an off-season for the colorful Berra, he still led all major league catchers in 1957 with 24 homers and 84 RBIs while fielding .995, highest mark for receivers in 100 or more games. Yogi, now a bowling alley proprietor along with Phil Rizzuto near Clifton, N. J., has a lifetime .290 batting mark and 1085 RBIs for his 11 full seasons as a Yankee. Three times, Berra has been named the Most Valuable Player in the American League and he's played on nine consecutive All-Star teams and he's been named All-Star major league catcher five times by the SPORTING NEWS.

BERRA, LAWRENCE PETER

Year	Club	G	AB	R	H	2B	3B	HR	RBI	BA	FA
1943	Norfolk	111	376	52	95	17	8	7	56	.253	.973
1944-45	Kansas City				(In Military Service)						
1946	Newark	77	277	41	87	14	1	15	59	.314	.972
1946	New York	7	22	3	8	1	0	2	4	.364	1.000
1947	New York	83	293	41	82	15	3	11	54	.280	.972
1948	New York	125	469	70	143	24	10	14	98	.305	.979
1949	New York	116	415	59	115	20	2	20	91	.277	.989
1950	New York	151	597	116	192	30	6	28	124	.322	.985
1951	New York	141	547	92	161	19	4	27	88	.294	.984
1952	New York	142	534	97	146	17	1	30	98	.273	.992
1953	New York	137	503	80	149	23	5	27	108	.296	.986
1954	New York	151	584	88	179	28	6	22	125	.307	.990
1955	New York	147	541	84	147	20	3	27	108	.272	.984
1956	New York	140	521	93	155	29	2	30	105	.298	.988
1957	New York	134	482	74	121	14	2	24	82	.251	.995
M. L. Totals		1474	5508	897	1598	240	44	262	1085	.290	.987

WORLD SERIES RECORD

Year	Club	G	AB	R	H	2B	3B	HR	RBI	BA	FA
1947	New York	6	19	2	3	0	0	1	2	.158	.920
1949	New York	4	16	2	1	0	0	0	1	.063	1.000
1950	New York	4	15	0	3	0	0	0	2	.200	1.000
1951	New York	6	23	4	6	1	0	0	0	.261	.968
1952	New York	7	28	2	6	1	0	2	3	.214	.985
1953	New York	6	21	3	9	1	0	1	4	.429	1.000
1955	New York	7	24	5	10	1	0	1	2	.417	1.000
1956	New York	7	25	5	9	2	0	3	10	.360	1.000
1957	New York	7	25	5	8	0	0	1	2	.320	.979
W. S. Totals		54	196	30	55	7	0	10	26	.281	.987

ALL-STAR GAME RECORD

Year	League	AB	R	H	2B	3B	HR	RBI	BA	FA
1949	American	3	0	0	0	0	0	0	.000	1.000
1950	American	2	0	0	0	0	0	0	.000	1.000
1951	American	4	1	1	0	0	0	0	.250	.857
1952	American	2	0	0	0	0	0	0	.000	1.000
1953	American	4	0	0	0	0	0	0	.000	1.000
1954	American	4	2	2	0	0	0	0	.500	1.000
1955	American	4	1	1	0	0	0	0	.167	1.000
1956	American	4	0	2	0	0	0	1	0.000	1.000
1957	American	3	0	1	0	0	0	0	.333	1.000
All-Star Game Totals		30	4	7	0	0	0	1	.233	.981

Yankee Stadium Then and Now

Old timers will long recount the greatness of the first stadium.
Aged men always speak this way. Yesterday's wars were harder.
Relief never came. Pain was sharper.
People had to be tougher, convictions, more firm.

Our time brushes off days of old.
We learn little from dead, white males.
The old stadium was just a ballpark with a short right field.
Murderer's Row a bunch of diminutive players
Who hit fast balls seldom exceeding eighty-six miles an hour.
Their fewer home runs prove today's athletes stronger
Despite original walls behind newer fences
Imagine Roger Bannister gaining notoriety for a four-minute mile.
A mark fit high schoolers can fulfil
Across the nations. Ah! Enough pointless comparisons.

Was there nothing impressive about the old timers,
Who won nineteen World Series, hit home runs

In huge ballparks and started rallies that took three or four
Batters to score a single run, saving home runs for the last course.
They may have no voice now, but they had presence.

There is evidence. Consider their hot dogs.
A scorched surface on a dry bun
Back then, the skin was very thin.
Even the mustard tasted sharper
Today's hot dogs are more modulated, moister.
The mustard — like the fans — milder.

The old signs at the Stadium wall did not change every minute
Less technology, singular message, more consistent,
Limited glitz. Selling the steak not the sizzle.
Spikes spiked. Rhubarbs bled. The dirt was authentic.
Umpires and managers more contentious
Old time players were always in your face.

Yesterday's fans had more toughness,
Sitting side-by-side in the sweltering bleachers.
Rough hands of carpenters and bricklayers,
Unblocked hats resting sideways on their heads.
Only a few private loges for the upper class.
Replaced by today's suit-wearing executives.
Endless guests of the Fortune 500 box seaters,
Enjoying expensive dinners,

Pushing the real fans to the upper decks or the bleachers.
Empty seats filled with deal makers and clients
Ignoring the game, digging in their briefcases.

Today's bombers rarely grit their teeth and beat out a bunt.
They use the haymaker swing and connect once a month
Less artful. No tricks. Too proud to wait for ball four
Three or four solo blasts replace
A free pass followed by an error to score.

Too much nonsense about size and power.
Baseball was never a big man's affair.
Think of Bobbie Shantz or Wee Willie Keeler
Yogi Berra, Phil Rizutto, Snuffy Stirnweiss,
The Babe hit with loft, eschewing the line drive
Imagine his prowess with today's adjusted fences,
He would set unattainable records.

In the old Stadium, the only thing was to win.
Nice guys finished last in the Polo Grounds and Brooklyn.
Smart guys finished first by fighting for every run
Nice guys only to the fans, especially kids.
Smiling, gladly signing their names.
So different from today's cool heroes
Who run past fans to the waiting limousines
On their way to the distant suburbs.

What is the greatest moment in American sports?
The 1969 Super Bowl where the underdog prevails?
The long count, as the challenger fell before landing a tirade of punches?
The American hockey team shocking the Russians?
How about Joe Louis and Max Schmeling.
Enemies for a time, friends later on.
A tale of two men. Two outcomes.
Two countries, two continents.
Symbolic of their turbulent times.

How about the Greatest Goodbye?
A rare moment transcending athletic victory
Touching on the meaning of a man's span of years
All ears fixed on the seven-time all-star.

Replaced by a bland community park,
It takes an old fan with a good memory to look
Beyond the goal posts and running track.

At River Avenue and 161st Street
You stand at a great crossroad.
Follow Yogi's advice: Take it!
And remember the great House
That helped build a small part of all of us.

The Science Fair

A magnet from two batteries and a wire
Toothpaste for dogs, spill-proof beaker,
A green furnace burning cedar.
Lighter fluid and coal spark the fire
The mold experiment came about without bother
Taken from the second shelf of Mom's refrigerator.
That diet is not new. Look in June's *Good
Housekeeping*.
Sounds like a recipe of Martha Stewart's conjuring.

Mom and Dad assemble the contraption
And show it proudly Saturday morning.
Hoping for the committee's recognition
Ensuring that a full college scholarship
Looms since junior cannot dribble or leap.

The School Science Fair — months in creation
The Scientific Method turned upside down
Where is the grey matter needed for an invention?
Tomorrow's Jobs? Gates? Fulton?
In this place, they sound like a double-play
combination.
The Principal says it starts here with us.

Kind Hearts are More than Coronets

Can anyone update Tennyson?
Is there even a sprinkling of ancient
Norman blood to compare with any kind heart?
In modern times, generosity has dried up.
Food stamps go by the softer name: SNAP
Welfare loses its power to bruise us
Now called simply Public Assistance.

No loss of dignity is permitted for the downtrodden.
Displaying their Nike Air Maxes
As a badge of distinction.
Alms are a thing of the past, rolled into taxes.
Collected by cold-hearted bureaucrats.
Stored in windowless federal vaults
Mailed to names on an endless list.
Verified by an audited review process.

No one says, "Thank you." No one says, "Please."
Government safety nets replace personal kindness and religious outreaches.
Generosity emanates from the secular taxpayer.
When cash is king, kind hearts are rare
'Tis only noble to be wealthy,
Ensuring you will qualify for an honorary degree.

Royalty has dwindled to a few clueless boobs
Wasting public funds, posing for photos
Smiling in their military uniforms,
Gawking from behind empty eyes
Never daring to don a crown or coronet.
That would not please the jet set.

If only Shaw could see all those who study
In colleges and all the cash ladled out for the good of humanity.
In the end they were right, the Fabian socialists.
We must do our best to wipe away ignorance.

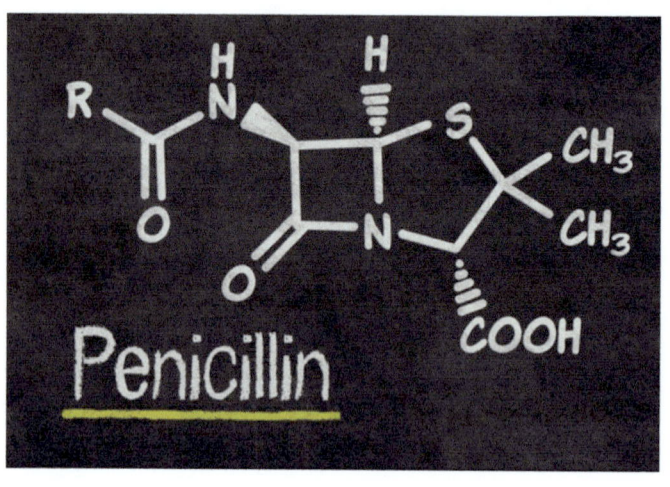

Penicillin Losing its Strength

The original antibiotic not working?
Try erythromycin or azithromycin
So many -ycins out there.
Gone too is yesteryear's towel and canister
Along with its etherized patient.

A pinch in the arm or the spine
Fills you with an anaesthetic just in time
Keep it flowing through the operation
Before the steady hand and the shank
Set the team on its surgical task
Watch the gauge for supply of oxygen.
That's the job of the medical technician.

Discomfort a source of concern?
Doctors never use the word pain.
Don't grit your teeth on the table. You'd be a fool.
Get a shot of fentanyl or propofol.
It would be a shame if they ran out of Diprivan
Just a quick stick for a trip to la-la land.

What a fortunate time to suffer a major illness.
Doctors use cat scans, monitors, transplants, miracle cures.
The test says your blood is too heavy, tends to clot?
More coagulated than polluted well water?
Didn't the Hatfields and McCoys
Settle which one really is thicker?
Back then, they did it with shotguns!
Try an anticoagulant such as heparin.
It's sure to make your blood thin.
Or atorvastatin, better known as Lipitor.
Have your doctor prescribe the latest cure.

Swelling in the feet? From water retention?
Pfizer always has the solution.
It's called flourisemide popularly called Lasix
Take the full dose when H_2O plays tricks.

So many pharmaceutical giants fighting for market share
This trend invigorates mighty AstraZeneca
Trying to outrace giant rival Takeda
In the search to make us all pain free
With no side effects. Just wait and see.

Worried about the financial burden?
The latest generics may ease the pain.
Pfizer's Chantix and Inlyta lose their patents
That's also a shame for Boehringer's Atrovent

Don't forget Bystolic from AbbVie and Pfizer's Sutent
Other newbies include Safyral from Bayer, parent of aspirin
Brings a smile to Tylenol maker, Johnson and Johnson
As well as Takeda's highly prized Uloric
Must also mention Vigamox from Novartis
All turning into cheaper commodities.
How that makes the investors frantic.

Need a vaccine at warp speed?
Who is going to seize the lead?
Could be Regeneron, Roche or Gilead.
Ask Pfizer and Moderna. All praise be
To Amgen, Glaxo Smith Kline, J&J and Sanofi
There's also BioNTech. Must include Oxford.
Poets step aside from these pastoral farms
Medical breakthroughs are being found
Amidst these plots of cottage ground.

More Horseradish

"Train to the suburbs? Look for track eight."
"Maryland? Oh, yes. Stops at Darnestown."
"The quiet car? Number Nine."
"Follow the man with the grey flannel suit."
Carrying the expensive leather case.
He came by government conveyance
The big white Mercedes in the handicap space.

Let's go home to our suburban community
Far from government forms and poverty
Where the gates are only for decoration
Not like the border of our nation
No discrimination in the entire area
Just ask Dr Shah, Dr Mohammad or Dr Aisha

It's been a hard day at the office.
So many need our labour and guidance.
All workers must earn their daily bread.
Remaining above it all, we must contend.

"Same menu they had before
At least they serve Johnny Walker.
Makes everything taste so much better."

Are they orange rinds at Table Three?
Getting fat is such a quandary.

"More horseradish for the prime ribs, sister?"
"Yes and Pinot Grigio. Or Pinot Noir."
"Benedictine brandy? Eggs Benedict with Hollandaise?"
"Let us remember, we are in the holy presence."

At least we dumped the Common Fund.
I still like Tesla, GM and Ford
Could have done better in a measly CD
I'd hate to be on the endowment committee
Should we buy Russian bonds or munis?
Have to separate the wheat from the chaff
Or, let them worry about it at Goldman Sachs.

We have to consider the giant hedge fund.
Must be socially conscious and pay high dividends.
No arms dealers or coal for our non-profit
We'll create a pile of scholarship cash for each applicant.

Our scholar athletes focus on academics.
They must develop their intellects.
Sports are so tough on the net net.
Title IX cuts deeply into our profit.
We make such a long, strenuous effort.
That goes for government employee and client.

If only taxpayers knew how we exert
For their benefit. We live on mere sustenance
As in earlier times — barely a pauper's pence,
We exist like an almsgiver or saint.
One must always remain resolute
The truth is, those we serve we barely tolerate.

The Great Toshi

A city reveals its own personality.
The great toshis of Japan face us in their way.
Less imposing, lacking bombast
They strike a chord in the visitor's heart.
Conveying the lives of their ancestors.

Kyoto stands out. More eerie, darker,
Eschewing the Ginza's glitter,
Colder than the sombre orange of Rome
That grabs hold of all who traverse its cobblestones
To weigh down the feet of centuries of pilgrims.
Absent are the mighty skyscrapers
Of modern era cities — New York, Chicago, London
Devoid of the grey clouds that hang over Dublin.

Bereft of financial centres and Canadian needles
And the trudging of millions in China's metropolises.
Look in vain for the fervent crowds of Mecca,
The exuberance of Times Square or Piccadilly Circus,
Or the echo that bounces through an empty basilica.

Kyoto exudes a feeling that lives were lived here.
Now complete, shadows force the new residents to inter

Their emotions and move reverently through the city.
Neater, smaller streets make Kyoto sadder,
Using its narrow pathways to wall in hearts.

Kyoto's past residents make their own imprint
On the present, setting up their town as a stopping point
In each great city's race to reach the heavens
Caretakers of heavy air that fills its streets
Reminding us that those who lived before us
Shape the arteries of all our lives.

A Viking Journey

Off they rowed, spurred by anger and violence
No man driven by these emotions thinks clearly.
The intrepid move on to satisfy a wild urge
No clear picture takes shape of how it will end
In the mind of such a crew of brutes.

Centuries before the boots marched through Europe
These fair skinned, big-shouldered roughnecks
Fulfilled their destiny, wild and bent on mayhem.

When the savagery started, they played their parts willingly
Long before that day, the Vikings went out with steady purpose
The quiet shores of Europe barely noticed the approaching boats
Unseen, a thrill went through each Einar, Ragnar and Hrothgar.
Over that small hill, behind those trees, across that valley
Some force would appear — surprised, disorganized, scurrying
Like squirrels or deer before a hunter.
Then the hacking began.

Stand behind the giant son of Ari who just last week
Was pulling fish from icy waters.
Men sliced, horses scattered.
Time to enter the village.
More aimless running around.
Women slamming doors.
Old men staring from upper floors.

The leader strokes his red beard. Time to seize
All we can. Doors forced open.
Plates, coins, food swept into new baskets
That only last week lay drying in the sun
At the river bank back home.
The select few carry young women.
The screamers smacked hard, laying limp
Across the shoulders of that special force.

Quick exit or slow exit? Red beard scans the horizon.
A few words to his private warrior band.
Loki, the coast guard, says his piece.
No enemy ships in sight. Away they row.
No riders on the shore. Another victory.
Enough for the long journey home
And a return to the repetitive tasks of
Tending the land and using up
The stores stashed at the mead hall
Before the next violent foray.

Old Toys

Has it really been fifty years since we played these games?
Checkers. So easy! Maybe fun for double jumps.
The short Scrabble words we argued over.
"Where's the dictionary?"
"Aha! Not there."
"Who's stockpiling Xs and Qs?"
There's the pencil worn to the short end
And the pocket watch with the missing hand
Ah, the sharp-edged Erector set.
Did success in Monopoly prognosticate
Our older brother's prowess in real estate?

How we ran to the closet to seize
The board games and smiled as we blew on the dice.
I drew that five decades ago?
Such a round face; the hair wild and indigo!
No Renoirs or Picassos in this family.
The smile was a good sign for my psyche.

Today's kids will have nothing to do with Grandma's board games
Or dining rooms for that matter or card tables.

Used to be we'd argue about Vietnam and entitlements.
No discussion at all these days.
Everyone on their smart phone zipping through photos.
Facebook friends trying for coy looks.
Cousins touting little Dakota's school projects.
"My child is straight A plus."

Electronic diversions may be quicker
No personal contact. No idle chatter.
Eyes and fingers fixed on the almighty computer
Even so, today's children are no smarter

Moore's Law still applies.
Computer chips get smaller and smaller.
Human hearts follow the electronics.
Despite these pointless forms of play,
Today's kids will reach their destiny
The gravy train will come their way.
They will enjoy the spoils as we did.
As today's athletes surpass the old timers
Today's youth will see themselves as better.

From the Wasteland

Burning rocks push up from below
Then the fiery mountain learns how
To protect itself. Unfriendly, windy and frozen at the peak
Shutting out the sun at least on one side.
Craggy, uneven, hard to climb.
Black and rocky, uninviting, wholly sublime.

The volcano's origin frightens, then it settles
Itself, aloof, ignoring mortals.
Until its rare, furious blasts
Set by the mountain's own timetable
Cool the earth better than any Paris deals.

Volcanoes form an angry band of brothers.
Suitable neighbours for Eric Bloodaxe and Freydis Eriksdottir.
Consider the family — Grisvotn, Blanjukur,
As well as Katla and Skjaldbreithur
Where any blow generates a mighty terror
Blocking the sun in this near Arctic, dewline land
Gushing smoke, fire and fear all around
Rattling its eastward neighbours.

As with all men bent on destruction,
Volcanoes and Vikings enjoy the heat
Of anger and revel in the thrill of domination.

Benignity

What is benignity? How long have I fretted over
This profound and troubling matter.
Can I feel a gift of the Holy Ghost?
Am I ever allowed to lose my temper?
Such an intense question!
Poems should offer the correct retort.

Like all great words, we know it first
In its dumbed-down form.
Niceness — a meaningless, general term
Sufficient for a B minus student.
Or for a remark one makes to a fiancé's parent.
"Of course you should have grandchildren."

Meteorological benignity is the end of rain,
A glimpse of the Northern Lights.
A sailor's soothing red sky at night,
Melting snow on a cold day in Saskatchewan,
Soft wind, safe voyage, tiny waves,
A Manitoba highway without snow flurries.

A quiet campus exemplifies serenity
Athletes in the locker room, following victory.

Students on a Friday night calling
The roller of big beer kegs
Before they mess up the tapping.

Cities exude tranquillity before break of day.
Copland captured the essence in *Quiet City*.
Soft rain deadens street sounds. Snow melts quickly
After its fall makes traffic halt.
Kids away at camp means summer quiet.
The wealthy roam the beach in the Hamptons
Or the Vineyard. Others run through hydrants.

Dante knew the deeper significance.
How far we have veered from the discarded image.
Belief in the unseen demands too great a charge.
Our world thirsts for scientific evidence.

Benignity pierces the human soul
Like the eyes in a Fra Angelico scene
Seeking you out through the paint on the monastery wall
And the centuries that intervene.

Here we stand of two minds, one scientific, sifting the evidence
Demanding petri dish confirmation if it ever comes clear
The other clinging to blind faith. At the summit, God unseen.

With such a spiritual fissure, justice will not roll like water
Or righteousness flow like a mighty stream.
How can we rail against previous eras of human existence.

The Deadline

It's four a.m. Must meet the lawyers.
Will they sign off? The deadline looms.
Our president needs to concur
Doesn't like to be 'disturbed'. Safely in bed.
Is that our counsellor
Or theirs busy on Zoom?

Must get home. Which private car is mine?
Limousine? Ha! Name plates on taxis!
Ten waiting at each door. Good sign for profits.
Everyone is borrowing and building.

All of this for our penniless client.
Ran out of funds a year back
Plans to build a Colossus of Roads
Down south somewhere, rural Texas
Just think of how much they will make
After we get the gelt.

Remember the ordeal of due diligence?
Lawsuits, falling revenue, rising expenses
Expired rights. Hate to be their attorneys.
Wouldn't be a pleasant experience.

All that glitters is not low risk, Triple A
Gone are the days of a Jimmy Carter Ginnie Mae
These bonds really can be called junk
So many risks. We need investors with spunk
Could be a great addition to someone's portfolio
As long as they avoid a major fiasco.

I'll never see these financiers again
Back to Broad Street or Hoboken or Austin
Just another tombstone for the front desk
Bonus for the top muckety-muck.

The controller is meeting the lawyers
I wait patiently at the accountant's office.
Blurred vision from so many sleepless nights.
When I sign, will my hand quiver?
Remember, this is Wall Street.
No decency in this business!

Bad Times for Theologians and Investors

In our days, an invisible cloud covers
Clear thinking and doctrine
Bad times for investor and theologian
Overvalued stocks and undervalued believers.
We drift from striving, saving and personal fervour.
Chariots of fire replaced by golden Land Rovers.

Unions grow where money flows
In Washington not on heartland farms
Statistics prove that learning excels
Inside crowded metropolitan schools.

Cancel culture eats up good deeds
That lie interred within ancestors' bones.
Within the human heart
Conviction turns more shaky.
Wisdom finds no sanctuary.

The Rogers Peet suit shields fund managers
From overseeing Christmas savings plans and IRAs.
Lunch at Fraunces Tavern fills brokers
With the vitamins of high returns.

Volatility worries investors and soon-to-be retirees.
Just consider Tesla's Model X
Sailing along, then knocked off its apex
By those clever Germans from Volkswagen.
Market cap drops like a quail dying
The Thomas Edisons of the electric auto
World find their wealth swirling
In a sudden financial tornado.
The great Musk loses his appeal
While believers lose their zeal.

Is God watching over our deeds?
Does he hear and answer prayers?
Older voices affirm this to be so.
We could all use a dose in this vale of woe.

So many faiths to entice us
Sophomorically said to be totally equal.
Some expect the golden streets of Paradise.
Others think life has no sequel
Despite vast differences in creed
Among so many disparate voices
Even defining good and evil finds few agreed
Let alone any purpose for our existence.

How fares the soul at the end of our days?
It used to be that a bad soul could redeem itself
Through penance and good deeds
Before the light fades

Not by raging against the dying of the light
Through actions that repair and change.
But now darkness envelopes us through the pilgrimage
We see no tunnel, no light at the exit.

In our time, wealth invigorates the masses
Just ask our forebearers or Eastern Europeans
Who yearned for riches across the bleak decades
As do the BRICS and all emerging nations.
Consider the power of financial sanctions.
The UN debates and votes in favour
As money replaces declarations of war.

Read the *Wall Street Journal*, the *Financial Times*.
You'll find the truth for these days.
See the high performing stocks and bonds
Select the shares about to ascend
Buy low, sell high is the way to proceed.

Will the portfolio centre hold
As life approaches the end?
Long before our funds terminate
We run out of faith.

Goodness and kindness are out of favour
Replaced by a new type of fervour.
Almsgiving gives way to wealth management.
How will the future lay out?
Worry, doubt and disappointment.

Follow today's easy route.
As was the case for our less wealthy ancestors,
Fuel your actions by the wisdom buried in human hearts.
Only the wise understand: those who went before us
Did not pine in darkness.

E Pluribus Unum

Blackout, manhole explosion, murder
Virus deaths, fire alarms, news of war.
How strangely big city residents react.
Some hurry their step. Others go about their rounds
In the manner of an angry halfback, lowered heads
Untouched, *sans* empathy, alone in their own circuit.

More focus is found at Union Station
On the first of the month when tickets expire.
The evening news blabs on from Washington
Stimulating a brief remark before slumber.

So many in a large country. All with diverse lives.
Factions ready to perform all kinds of tasks:
Caring for the sick, mortal combat, safe street crossing,
Vaccine injections, election day poll watching.
Such a peculiar smattering
Of people with divergent
Views and lives that rarely connect.

What unites us who proceed without common beliefs?
Work? Living nearby? Thriving economy?
But we move along, better than the closely

Linked people of smaller, poorer nations.

What a strange world to embrace so many billions.
Where the best proceed from inner convictions.
The worst use any ploy to vent their anger
Shared momentarily with a fellow conspirator.

Times Past

What is it about years ago that intrigues us?
So sweet and comforting in today's tribulation.
Riots, war, conflict, the want of human consolation
Are lost in the stasis of memories.
All becomes pleasant and dreamy
Sorry, Marc, evil is oft interred within the bones
Of the dead. Their goodness remains.
It was so in your time. Let it be with us.